MODERN CURRICULUM PRESS

The Computer Rules

Alvin Granowsky
Joy Ann Tweedt
Craig L. Tweedt
Illustrated by Michael L. Denman

MCP

MODERN CURRICULUM PRESS
Cleveland • Toronto

© **1985 MODERN CURRICULUM PRESS, INC.**
13900 Prospect Road, Cleveland, Ohio 44136.

Softcover edition published simultaneously in Canada by Globe/
Modern Curriculum Press, Toronto.

Library of Congress Cataloging in Publication Data

Granowsky, Alvin, 1936-
    The computer rules.

    Summary: A family enjoys its new computer so much that meals,
homework, and other important things are neglected, so the family
members decide to make some rules.
    1. Children's stories, American. (1. Computers — Fiction.
2. Family life — Fiction)   I. Tweedt, Craig, 1950-   .
II. Tweedt, Joy, 1951-   .   III. Denman, Michael L., ill.
IV. Title.
PZ7.G76664Co   1985   (E)   84-8982

ISBN 0-8136-5143-3 (hardcover)
ISBN 0-8136-5643-5 (paperback)

1 2 3 4 5 6 7 8 9 10   86 85 84

"What is in the boxes?
Is it a puppy for me?" asked Amy.
"Maybe it is a bike for me,"
said Steve.

5

"Look what I have!" said Father.
"It is a computer.
We can work and play with the
computer."

6

"Oh!" said Steve.
"We have a computer at school!
I love to use the computer!"

7

"I was hoping for a puppy," said Amy.

"Let me use the computer," said Steve.
"Let me play a game now."

"No," said Father.
"I need to use the computer now.
I have work I need to do."

her said, "It is time for dinner!"
ease eat dinner with us!"
Amy and Steve.

11

Father did not eat dinner.
He worked with the computer.

He worked with it.
And he worked with it.
"I love to work with the
computer!" he said.

The next day Steve ran to the computer.
"Now I can play with the computer."

14

"No," Mother said.
"I need to use the computer now.
I have work I need to do."

Father said, "It is time for breakfast."
"Please eat breakfast with us!"
said Amy and Steve.

Mother did not eat breakfast.
She worked with the computer.
"I love to work with the computer."

"I want to play with the computer after school," said Steve.

"I want a puppy," said Amy.
"I could play with it all the time."

19

"Mother, we are home from school.
Can I use the computer now?"
asked Steve.

"Yes," said Mother.
"You can use the computer.
But you must do your
homework, too!"

"I will do my homework, Mother.
I will do it after I play with
the computer."

Steve did not do his homework.
He worked with the computer.
"I love to work with the computer!"

The next day at
breakfast Father asked,
"Do you have your
homework?"

"He did not do it!" said Amy.

"I did not do it," said Steve.

"I did not eat dinner!" said Father.

"I did not eat breakfas[t]" said Mother.

"I did not do my homework!"
said Steve.

"I did not play with the
computer!" said Amy.

"We have a problem!" said Mother

"Yes," said Father. "We have a problem with the computer."

"What can we do?" asked Steve.

28

"We need rules!" said Amy. "At school we have rules for using the computer."

29

"That is what we will do!" said Father.

"Yes," said Mother. "We will make rules for using the computer!"

"Amy, your rules will help us!" said Father.
"Do we need rules for your puppy, too?"

THE COMPUTER RULES

Word Count: 77
Readability: 1.6

a	eat	make	said
after		maybe	school
all	Father	me	she
Amy	for	mother	Steve
and	from	must	
are		my	that
asked	game		the
at		need	time
	have	next	to
bike	he	no	too
boxes	help	not	
breakfast	his	now	us
but	home		use(ing)
	homework	oh	
can	hoping		want
computer		play	was
could	I	please	we
	in	problem	what
day	is	puppy	will
did	it		with
dinner		ran	work(ed)
do	let	rules	
	look		you
	love		your
			yes